To:

From:

Copyright © 2009 Hallmark Licensing, Inc.

Published by Hallmark Books,
a division of Hallmark Cards, Inc.,
Kansas City, MO 64141
Visit us on the Web at www.Hallmark.com.

Editorial Director: Todd Hafer
Editor: Megan Langford
Art Director: Kevin Swanson
Designer: Mark Voss
Production Artist: Dan Horton

ISBN: 978-1-59530-029-4

BOK3093

Printed and bound in China

GIFT BOOKS
from Hallmark

She believed she could
so she did.

**Life is either
a daring adventure
or nothing.**

HELEN KELLER

While you live, *love.*

While you breathe, *sing.*

While you walk, *dance.*

While you work, *shine.*

While you see, *dream.*

Some days are hopscotch kind of days, some days are getting-nailed-at-dodgeball kind of days.

Nothing is insignificant.

SAMUEL T. COLERIDGE

I *believe* in the power of positive bitching.

Love strong.

If only **emotional baggage** came with those cute little **emotional wheelies.**

Happy will always find you.

Through love, through friendship,
A heart lives more than one life.

ANAIS NIN

That little voice in your head that says, **go buy shoes,** that's the one to listen to.

Half of doing
is believing that you can.

Follow your heart.
It knows the way.

Wherever you are,

you shine.

More *dreaming,*
less worry.

More *ease,*
less chaos.

More *fun,*
less work.

More *time,*
more *laughter,*
more *love.*

Hope for the best.
Plan for the worst.
Snack in between.

Friendship? Yes, please.

CHARLES DICKENS

Sometimes you just gotta *go all out* and put two sugars in your coffee.

Scatter joy.

RALPH WALDO EMERSON

There just aren't
enough lunch hours
in the day.

Live happy.

The ^real^ To-Do List

- Sing.
- Smile at strangers.
- Keep learning.
- Notice kindness.
- Eat ice cream.
- Hope.
- Count your blessings.
- Laugh.
- Love.
- Love some more.

I have hope
and I'm not afraid to use it.

It's often the bend in the road that makes life **worth the drive.**

Dreams
have no expiration date.

Chocolate
won't solve anything
but it's a fine place to start.

To thine own self be *nice.*

See the good
all around you,
even if you have
to squint.

Every *flower* **that blooms**
has to go through a whole lot of *dirt.*

You can never have
too much *happy.*

She listened to her *heart* and that made all the difference.

Let it be.

Faith is hope on fire.

Be where you are.
Otherwise, you will miss your life.

BUDDHA

When the chips are down,
bring on the cheese dip!

I take it
one day at a time,
but sometimes several of them
attack me at once.

There's no problem
that friends cannot
confront, combat, plot against,
ignore, make fun of,
drown in chocolate sauce
or run over with the car.

Make today a day for *the fancy toothpicks.*

Good things come
to those who love.

Imagine.

**All you've got
is all you can give
and that will**
always
be enough.

Be yourself.
Everybody else is already taken.

OSCAR WILDE

**Take every chance
to relax,
to hope,
to heal,
to dream,
to play,
to give,
to receive . . .**

to love.

We all need someone
who gives us the *courage*
to be who we're meant to be.

Never stop
being curious.

The stuff that wears on the nerves
polishes the soul.

You never know what good things
will pour in when the heart is open to life.

Do what you love—
it's what you were meant to do.

If you have *no regrets,*
you need to get out more.

Life isn't perfect,
but love doesn't care.

To see yourself through the eyes of a friend
is to know how special you really are.

Life is too important
to be taken seriously.

OSCAR WILDE

It's not the things we do in life that wear us down.

It's what we don't do.

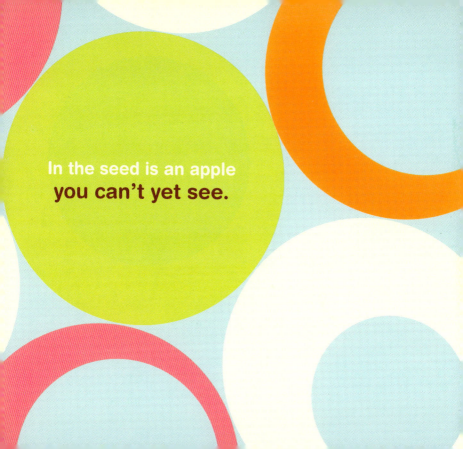

In the seed is an apple
you can't yet see.

Hang in there.

Even the worst weeks have Fridays in them.

If the tiara fits, *wear it.*

It's not the journey or the destination.
It's the seatmate.

It's a **rare person**
who can take care
of **hearts**
while also taking care
of **business.**

The best way *out*
is always *through.*

The tide *always* turns.

LOL
is not the answer to everything.
But most things.

If at first you don't succeed . . .
pretend you weren't really trying.

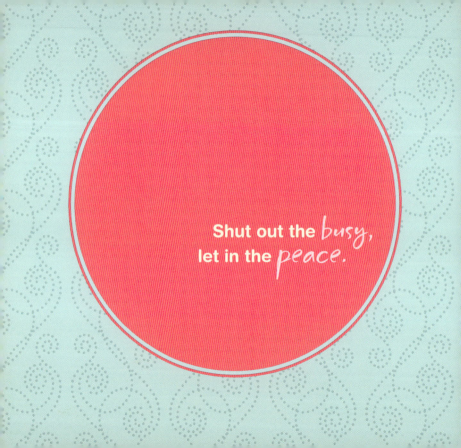

Shut out the busy,
let in the peace.

Anyone who has never made a mistake

has never tried anything new.

ALBERT EINSTEIN

Birds in the skies.
Limes in the drinks.
All is good in the world.

That which does not kill me
makes me want to eat *a cookie.*

Laugh louder.

Even the *stuff* that has to get done
doesn't have to get done *today.*

Many people walk in and out of your life
but only true friends will leave footprints on your heart.

ELEANOR ROOSEVELT

A little bit of reckless abandon

is a good thing.

Every time a door closes,
another opens somewhere else.
I think it's, like, an air pressure thing.

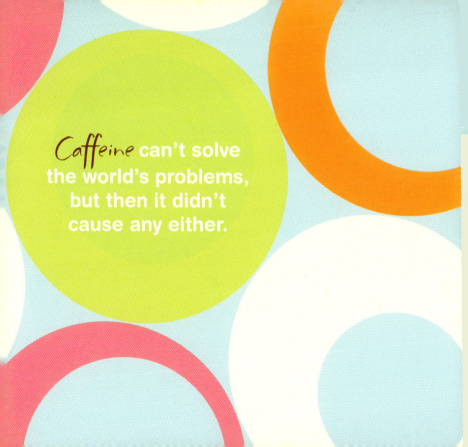

Caffeine can't solve
the world's problems,
but then it didn't
cause any either.

"Seize the day!"
does not necessarily have to include
the morning part of the day.

Joy.
Jump for it.

A real friend

knows when to *listen,*
when to stop listening,

when to *talk,*
when to stop talking,

when to *pour wine,*
when to stop pouring
and just *hand over the bottle.*

Dream no small dream.

VICTOR HUGO

Never put away your *dancing shoes.*

If you have enjoyed this book
or it has touched your life in some way,
we would love to hear from you.

Please send your comments to:
Hallmark Book Feedback
P.O. Box 419034
Mail Drop 215
Kansas City, Missouri 64141

Or e-mail us at:
booknotes@hallmark.com